To

_____

From

_____

Date

_____

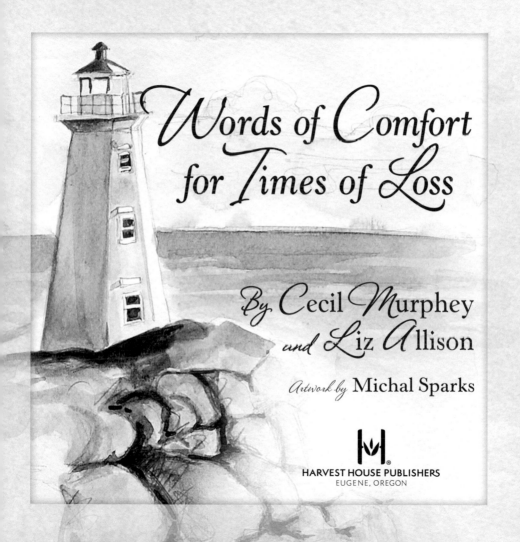

Words of Comfort for Times of Loss

By Cecil Murphey
and Liz Allison

Artwork by Michal Sparks

HARVEST HOUSE PUBLISHERS
EUGENE, OREGON

Words of Comfort for Times of Loss

Text Copyright © 2010 by Cecil Murphey and Liz Allison
Artwork Copyright © 2010 by Michael Sparks

Published by Harvest House Publishers
Eugene, Oregon 97402
www.harvesthousepublishers.com

ISBN 978-0-7369-2429-0

Mr. Gifford B. Bowne II
Indigo Gates
1 Pegasus Drive
Colts Neck, NJ 07722
(732) 577-9333

Design and production by Garborg Design Works, Savage, Minnesota

Printed in China

17 18 19 20 21 / FC / 10 9 8 7 6 5

A note to our readers:
Though we are two individuals dealing with loss in
different ways, we came together and wrote with one voice
from one heart to share with you in your time of loss.
Cec and Liz

Contents

Why We Write About Loss

On the morning of July 12, 1993, my husband, Davey, left home like any other morning—he kissed my forehead and hugged our kids. That afternoon I answered a knock at the door, sensing something wasn't quite right. When I glanced at the faces of Davey's two close friends, they didn't have to speak—the looks on their faces said it all.

That day, after lunch with his race team, Davey hopped into his helicopter for an unplanned trip to the nearby Talladega Superspeedway to watch a buddy race. Attempting to land in the infield, he lost control of his helicopter and crashed. Although paramedics airlifted Davey to a Birmingham hospital, sixteen hours later he was pronounced dead.

Immediately following Davey's death, I had to work through my grief enough to plan his funeral and make hundreds of small-but-significant decisions, all while maintaining the time and energy to care for our two young children, ages one and three. Well-wishing friends hovered around me and frequently asked, "What can I do for you?"

Most of the time, I could only respond with a blank stare. Looking back, my friends could have done many things for me, but they didn't know what to do, and I didn't know what to tell them.

I hope the insights I have gained during the aftermath of Davey's death will help you as you struggle with your own grief.

That's why we've written this book.

—Liz

Two weeks after my father suffered a ministroke, a massive stroke took his life. On the day of his funeral, my older brother, Ray, died of cancer. Over the next eighteen months, I lost two brothers-in-law and my mother.

On the Sunday after Dad's and Ray's funerals, a parishioner rushed up to me, hugged me, and said, "Pastor, I heard about the deaths. Were they saved?"

I honestly don't remember what I answered, but I wanted to shout, "Does it matter right now? I hurt. I'm so filled with pain that I'm not sure I can handle the worship service today!"

In 2007, our house burned down. Our son-in-law, Alan, died in the fire. The next day, a neighbor pulled up in front of our burned house, got out of his car, and started to look around. "Where did he die?" he asked.

Through the years, I've met many like those two people. Maybe they didn't know what to say. Perhaps they were so focused on what they cared about that they were unaware of my pain. Instead of helping me, those comments made me feel even worse. What I needed was compassion. I didn't get that from either of them, but I can offer it to you.

That's why we've written this book.

– Cec

6

7

1
Little Joys

No one grieves the way you do. Your grief is private and intimate. As you've probably already learned, healing from grief doesn't come immediately. Healing comes slowly. You can't rush it, but one day you'll be able to look back and realize you're better today than you were three days ago.

Healing happens in almost imperceptible ways. It often comes through little joys—those moments when you feel lifted beyond your pain; those brief interludes when peace fills your heart and you sense God's presence. Little joys are everywhere, but you have to be open to see them. You have to be open to embrace them.

Liz Allison found her little joys in nature. After the death of her husband, she walked alone every day. This gave her time to be by herself and clear her head. She stared in awe at the fresh colors of summer. She examined the maple leaves and marveled at the intricacy of God's creation. She paused to stare at the billowy clouds crawling across the horizon. Some days she walked briskly. Other days she paused to watch a squirrel jump from limb to limb in the pine trees. Little joys. Little steps toward healing.

After the loss of his son-in-law, Cecil Murphey continued his early morning running schedule—when it was dark and quiet. "God could speak to me in the silence," he said. During the first few minutes of his run, he decided he would focus on gratitude. No matter how deeply he hurt, he would give thanks to God for the little things in his life. Instead of thinking about his loss, he decided to focus on what he had gained. Neighbors and friends showered him with love, clothes, and money. Church friends brought food. Strangers sent cards and gifts. Little joys. Little moments when God felt close.

The night before Martin Freeman died

No matter how deeply he hurt, he would give thanks to God for the little things in his life.

from emphysema, his wife sat beside his hospital bed. "I won't be going home," he said. Betty began to cry, and he stopped her. "You're a tough old gal, and I want you to remember the good memories and not to focus on the bad. You won't be alone because God will be with you. When you start to think negatively, focus on good things."

When Betty felt sad, she focused on the good memories of the things they did together. "That always lifted my spirits," she said.

"I couldn't read my Bible," one man said, "but I could play the guitar." He said that when he felt the worst, he would let his fingers glide across the strings. For minutes at a time he transcended the loss of his only daughter. "I felt God's loving presence."

Julie Garmon's son lived twenty minutes after his birth. She found her joy in such simple things as noticing the buds on

You need those little joys.

the dogwood trees, listening to the crickets in the night, or gazing at the stars. Little joys. Little moments when she would feel the embrace of divine love.

No matter how deep your pain, you can discover the little joys. You can find those brief interludes that enable you to pull back from your pain. As you let that happen—even for a few brief seconds—each moment of joy becomes a moment of healing.

You need those little joys. Eventually they accumulate and become great joys.

Here's a word for you from Jesus. "I am leaving you with a gift—peace of mind and heart. And the peace I give is a gift the world cannot give. So don't be troubled or afraid" (John 14:27).

Dear God, thank you for little joys. Thank you for those brief moments when I sense your presence and can rise above my grief. Amen.

2

You're Not Alone

"You're not alone," the woman said before she hugged Cec Murphey and his wife. How many times have people said those words to you? They say such words because they care. They don't want you to hurt. They want you to know they're available to help you.

But they don't understand, do they?

You *are* alone. No matter how caring your friends or how compassionate your family, no one else in the world feels your loss the way you do. You can find many ways to deny or to ignore your loss. You probably have gotten good at faking the smile or saying thank you when you'd rather be alone and grieve in private.

You *feel* alone in your private grief. Despite the compassion and assurance, the words feel empty, and you want the hurt to go away.

You want life to be the way it was before. But you know that life can never be that way again, and you feel so alone.

I will never fail you. I will never abandon you.

You can admit that you're not the only person in the world who grieves, but right now you can't think about anyone else. *I hurt,* you say to yourself. Maybe the tears fall—maybe you hold them back. Maybe you feel your heart is so broken it will never heal.

Despite how you feel, Someone is with you. Even in the deepest moments of your grief and pain, Jesus Christ whispers, "I will never fail you. I will never abandon you" (Hebrews 13:5). You may not feel his presence, but he is there. The prophet Isaiah calls him "a man of sorrows, acquainted with deepest grief" (Isaiah 53:3). "You are not alone," he says. "Not ever."

Lord Jesus, I welcome your healing arms that engulf me. Dry my tears, calm my anxieties, and remind me that I'm not alone. Remind me often. Amen.

$\mathcal{I}$ wanted
someone to say,
"Here is how I
can help you."

18

3
One Simple Thing

For days after Liz's husband, Davey, died, it seemed all anyone could say to Liz was, "What can I do for you?"

If only they had realized that she had no idea what she needed. *If I don't know what to do for myself,* she thought, *how can I know what you can do for me?* She admitted that there were times she barely even knew her own name, much less what someone else could do for her.

Even though her friends and family meant well, their questions became a constant reminder of how lost she felt within herself during this time of insurmountable grief. Instead of *asking* what they could do for her, Liz realized that she needed someone to help her figure out what she did need and how friends and loved ones could help. "I wanted someone to say, 'Here is how I can help you.' I wanted someone to take over my life, to get inside my head and help me know what I needed."

*She said,
"I'll pray for you."
Just one sentence—
and she had
no idea what
that did for Liz.*

Liz wanted to mourn, but with all that needed to be done, this was becoming increasingly difficult to do. What she really wanted was her husband back. She wanted her life back the way it was before the accident. But the one thing she knew she wanted was the one thing no one could give her.

In looking back, Liz realizes her friends and loved ones only wanted to help but really didn't know how to, which made them feel inadequate. They cared deeply and tried to express in their own way their kindness and sympathy. Perhaps asking her what they could do made *them* feel as if they had at least tried and somehow helped her.

By contrast, two days after she buried Davey, she had a rare period of quiet time. She felt totally vulnerable, and fear filled her mind. *What will I do without Davey? How can I raise two children on my own? Who will take care of me?* Tears rolled down her cheeks.

A dear friend was in the other room and must have heard her crying. She came to her side and took her hand. The friend spoke one sentence to her. She said, "I'll pray for you." Just one sentence—and she had no idea what that did for Liz.

That one thing—that one simple thing—was

the first true healing moment in Liz's recovery.

The friend didn't *ask* if she could pray. She just did it. Liz hardly heard the words, but her emotions surfaced, and she felt as if her soul had been poured out. When the friend had finished praying, Liz said it was as if her tears had washed away all the immediate pain. "I couldn't even whisper a word of thanks. All energy had been drained from my body. I was at peace for the first time in days."

Liz knew that there would be other days with more pain and more tears, but none like that one. On that day Liz learned an invaluable lesson: When people are grieving, they rarely know what they want or need.

Perhaps you're where Liz was that day. Your friends obstruct your grief by asking questions you can't answer. If only they would trust their instincts and do what they know they can do—like Liz's friend. She did that one simple, yet powerful, thing and brought peace in the midst of grief—she prayed.

Lord, help me. I hurt and don't know what I need. Give my friends and loved ones the wisdom to pray for me and to know how to help me. Keep them from asking me questions I can't answer. Amen.

22

4

Accepting Help

"After weeks of ignoring offers of assistance from well-wishers," Liz said, "a good friend insisted I needed help, and she was going to help me figure out exactly what I needed. That was one of the best gifts a friend could have given me—a gentle but firm intervention."

Together they figured out what had to be done around the house, what needed to be done for the kids, and what legal matters had to be handled— such as the death certificate and life insurance policy. They also figured out what Liz needed personally. The friend placed the weekly Liz-needs-to-do list on the refrigerator so that Liz would be reminded that people cared and wanted to help. Most important, Liz learned that she couldn't do it all herself and that she needed the assistance they offered.

As difficult as it may be for you to graciously receive help from others, remember that the Bible makes it clear that God wants us to

Accepting assistance is not a sign of weakness. It is simply allowing others to share your load.

ask for his help. The Bible also makes it apparent that we need each other, and at no time is that more obvious than during times of bereavement.

"So let's not get tired of doing what is good… Therefore, whenever we have the opportunity, we should do good to everyone—especially to those in the family of faith" (Galatians 6:9-10).

We're also told, "Be happy with those who are happy, and weep with those who weep" (Romans 12:15).

God doesn't intend for you to struggle with your losses without his help or without the help of the ones who love and care for you. Accepting assistance is not a sign of weakness. It is simply allowing others to share your load.

Receiving help is also a way to honor and encourage those who offer. It's as if you say, "I want you to know how important you are to me. I'll accept your help because I know you love me."

Lord, you know leaning on others and accepting help is difficult for me. Yet I know that if the situation were reversed, I would want to do something for the hurting people I love. Help me give others the chance to show their love to me. Amen.

*No one can tell you
how to grieve or give
you a painless way to
work through it.*

5

Make It Go Away!

"*I* want the hurting to stop!"

"I can't take more pain!"

"I'll never be happy again. My world has been destroyed."

"If only…if only I could make people understand the hurt."

Have you said some of these things? Grief isn't easy to go through. It turns your orderly life into one of chaos. The more deeply you love, the more painful your grief.

No one can tell you how to grieve or give you a painless way to work through it. You have to take your own personal journey into those dark and unknown places. Accept it as a fact that no one feels exactly the way you do. Others have grieved as deeply—perhaps even

God didn't take away the pain, but he held my hand while I went through it.

more deeply—but that doesn't mean they know precisely how you feel, even if they say they do.

It might seem as if crying out for the pain to go away makes its grip even tighter. Someone once said that the only way *out* of the pain is *through* the pain. As you face your grief, allow yourself to feel it, and you will begin to recover.

If you can't take "one day at a time," take one hour or even one minute at a time. Give yourself permission to cry, to go to bed, to lie in the darkness without a light. Do whatever you need to do for yourself. We suggest that you find ways to get alone where you can fall to pieces. Most people can't bear to watch you fall apart, and they want to rush in and take away your pain. Don't let them.

Get away from everyone. Scream. Cry. One man got into his car, rolled up the windows, and yelled as he drove across town. He came back hoarse, but his spirit was lighter. A woman said, "I told everyone to leave me alone for an hour. I went into my bedroom and locked the door. I lay face-down on my bed and cried. I'm not a screamer, but the tears were so heavy I had to change the pillowcase." Both of these people felt relief. In their own way, they did something for their own healing.

Turning to the God of comfort, one man said, "For days I couldn't express any feelings. At best I moaned 'Oh Lord, oh Lord.' " A friend spoke candidly, "God didn't take away the pain, but he held my hand while I went through it."

A woman said she found comfort in reciting Psalm 23:4 several times a day: "Yea, though I walk through the valley of the shadow of death, I will fear no evil; for You are with me; Your rod and Your staff, they comfort me" (NKJV).

God of love and compassion, right now I hurt, and I want it to go away. Maybe it will one day. Ease my inner pain, O Lord. Touch me with your love and enable me to sense that you are truly with me. Amen.

God wants to be your comforter.

30

6

Why Did You Leave Me?

*T*hat's not a rational question, but it's a realistic one. Some have expressed it this way: Why didn't I die first?

Those words contain a mixture of anger, pain, and fear. Don't be afraid to admit to yourself how you feel, even if the emotions seem irrational. It's all right to feel those emotions. They express who you are at that moment. Your emotions will fluctuate—you may cry one minute, find something hilariously funny the next, and in ten minutes feel entirely different yet again. What you feel is more important than what makes sense or whether others understand.

Don't be afraid to admit to yourself how you feel.

It's all right to feel anger and to express it aloud. Talk to the person you lost:

- You left me with three children to raise on my own. I'm angry and I'm afraid.

- I had wonderful plans for you. I wrapped my life around you. Now you're gone, and I have no life left.

- You were the only person I ever truly loved in my life.

- Why couldn't we have died together? I feel as if I've been sentenced to a life of unrelenting pain.

For this stage of your grief, accept your feelings. Cec often says, "My feelings are emotions—they are not reality." He uses that statement as a way to acknowledge his feelings, especially the negative ones.

Too many people don't want you to feel angry. They can't handle it when you yell out that life isn't fair or that you're mad because he died and left you alone.

Why did you leave me? It's okay to ask this because the question doesn't demand an answer. It may be an expression of anger. It might be a cry from someone who feels desolate and alone. It could be an expression of the deeper question, *How can I survive without you?* Or it may be a way of saying, *I depended on you, and you let me down. You died.*

Irrational? Of course, but they're still your feelings. Even if God gave you five reasons for the death of your loved one, it wouldn't make any difference. The person is still gone. Your pain is still with you.

But the pain is temporary. God wants to be your comforter. The psalmist wrote, "The LORD is close to the brokenhearted; he rescues those whose spirits are crushed" (Psalm 34:18).

God, sometimes my thinking doesn't make sense to me. Sometimes my loss clouds my reasoning. But I know you understand, and I know you're with me even in such dark, confusing times. Amen.

7

If Only I Had...

"If only I had insisted he go to the doctor earlier."

"If only I had been kinder and realized how sick she was."

"If only I had paid attention to the signs of her deep depression."

"If only…" You can fill in your own conclusion to this sentence. Most of us have regrets when we face loss. It's natural to focus on what we did wrong, the things we neglected to do, or the harsh words we said. It's natural to take the blame for attitudes and actions that really would have made no difference in the outcome.

It's all right to have regrets. It's all right to yearn for what might have been. This is the time to sort things out—a time to discover the difference between what is realistic and what's impossible. Naturally, you are finding yourself overwhelmed with a load of emotions, trying

to straighten them out, and doing your best to get past them.

But instead of trying to get past them, realize that in time the power of those emotions will diminish. Think of those feelings this way: *They are what I feel now. For right now, this is what I need to feel.* Too often we want to turn off our feelings or bury them. Instead, consider that divine wisdom is at work, urging you to believe that this is a true feeling—and accept it.

Cec has this theory, "I need to feel what I feel." He believes that the feeling represents something with which he needs to cope with his grief. Liz leans on her own saying, "I am where I am," to ground herself and to accept where she is emotionally at that moment.

It's all right to have regrets. It's all right to yearn for what might have been.

37

Whatever your emotions, tell yourself that it's all right to feel them.

Perhaps it's something you haven't faced yet…or might need to face again. The negative emotion has come to the surface so you can feel it, cope with it, and grow from the experience. The more readily you can accept your feelings as genuine and that it's all right to feel the way you do, the sooner you will move toward peaceful acceptance of every emotion.

Here's an example. "I never cried after I was about ten years old," one man said. "I didn't think I knew how to cry. Then came the loss of my son in an accident. I began to cry, and I didn't think I would ever stop. I cried over more than my son's death, even though that devastated me. I was also crying for all the pain I had tried to hide from myself."

He needed to cry, and he did. You may need to feel anger, resentment, or guilt. Whatever your emotions, tell yourself that it's all right to feel them. You may even need to say to yourself, "This is the way I need to feel right now."

Perhaps the words of this psalm will comfort you: "How can I know all the sins lurking in my heart? Cleanse me from these hidden faults" (Psalm 19:12). As you open yourself to God and to your feelings, think of these words: "I know the LORD is always with me. I will not be shaken, for he is right beside me" (Psalm 16:8).

Dear God, I don't like the emotions that are stirred up inside of me. I want them to go away. But I also know that I need to feel them—no matter how painful they may be. Grant me your strength to go through this ordeal. Amen.

8

What's Wrong with Self-pity?

"You've been moping around here and feeling sorry for yourself long enough," a mother said to her widowed daughter. "You need to start living again."

Feeling sorry for herself? Yes, she did. Some would call it self-pity. That's probably true. But isn't self-pity another word for grief? When you lose someone you love, you think of yourself. You remember life the way it was. You cringe at the future and wonder how you can possibly go on. They're gone. You'll never see them again; never hear their voice or feel their touch. You mourn for them. That's feeling sorry for yourself. *That is self-pity.* And it's all right.

Self-absorption—thinking only of yourself—can reach an unhealthy state, and that does happen. But for now—for the time of

Don't try to hurry
through the pain.

Allow others
to comfort you.

42

grief—give yourself permission to think about yourself, your loss, your pain.

Don't try to hurry through the pain. Take the necessary time to deal with your loss. There is no magic number of days to grieve, and there is no specific number of times to cry. Allow others to comfort you. Give them the opportunity to wrap their arms around you and shower you with compassion.

Never forget that Jesus, too, cried. When he was with the mourners, just before going to the grave of his friend Lazarus, the Bible says in the simplest words, "Then Jesus wept" (John 11:35). If Jesus can weep, so can you.

God, right now I feel sorry for myself. I feel as if I'm the most lonely, miserable person in the world. I don't want anyone to tell me about the pain of others or that others may hurt worse than I do. Right now I can focus only on my own pain. Thank you for letting me have this time to feel sorry for myself. Amen.

*C*ry out to your loving God and feel his holy embrace. He will help you move through the dark nights of sadness.

44

9

Perfect Grieving

"*I* wanted to grieve perfectly," Julie Garmon said when she spoke about the death of her newborn son. "I wanted my grief to be quick. I held it inside and told myself I didn't feel the pain. I didn't want to talk about it, and I didn't want anyone to talk to me about my loss. I didn't want to involve anyone else. They have their own lives, I reminded myself. I just want to put this all behind me. I don't need to be crying and making other people sad.

"I did all the good, Christian things. I focused on gratitude. I tried to think of dozens of things every day and give thanks to God. As a Christian, how could I be sad and still praise God? In my mind, such mixed feelings couldn't coexist. Christians praise God and read their Bibles and tell others about all their spiritual victories. That's what

His desire to rush through his grief was a form of running away from the pain.

I did. I read and quoted verses such as, 'Always be joyful. Never stop praying. Be thankful in all circumstances, for this is God's will for you who belong to Christ Jesus' (1 Thessalonians 5:16-18).

"I wanted an A-plus on my grieving report card. By the time I went for my six-week checkup, I expected to be over all that grief. At least a year passed before I could honestly acknowledge I was healed."

Cec understood Julie because his experience was similar. "I want to be finished with my grieving," Cec said to a friend four weeks after the deaths of his dad and his brother. "This has gone on long enough." He had given himself about a month and thought that by then he ought to have worked through all the stages of grief and should be healed. He wasn't.

Cec had to learn that he couldn't hurry the grief process. In fact, his desire to rush through his grief was a form of running away from the pain. If he could convince himself that he was past the grief, he wouldn't feel it. "I didn't want to hurt," he says. "I didn't want to feel anything to distract me. I'd watch TV and start to cry over some seemingly insignificant statement or scene."

No one can push you through your grief—and you, in particular, shouldn't do that to yourself. Cry out to your loving God and feel his holy embrace. He will help you move through the dark nights of sadness.

Perfect God, I realize there is no perfect way to grieve. Help me feel my pain in my own way. But most of all, please give me a sense of your presence during this dark period. Amen.

For those who grieve, the emotional ups and downs are one of the most difficult things to deal with.

10

Am I Crazy?

"Why don't I feel like myself anymore? One minute I am sad, the next I am angry. How can that be? Why can't I shake these overwhelming emotions? Will I ever be the old me again?"

These are all questions that most of us face. They ran through Liz's mind so often that fear became a reality for her. "I feared that life as I knew it would never be again. What if the *me* that once existed would never be *me* again? If only someone had told me this roller coaster of emotions is normal when we grieve—it wouldn't have taken away the pain, but it would have calmed the uneasiness as I tried to figure out if, in addition to my grief, I was going crazy."

Am I losing my mind? That question struck Liz many, many times. As Liz would learn, for those who grieve, the emotional ups and downs are one of the most difficult things to deal with. How could it be possible

It's all right to be you, and it's all right to feel exactly the way you do.

to cry buckets of tears one minute and laugh hysterically the next and, somewhere in the middle of the tears and laughter, to discover feelings of anger toward the loved one who died?

Because of the influx of emotions that come with grieving, it is easy to feel unlike yourself and even to think you're losing your mind. Liz discovered that the best gift she could give herself was to accept the emotions as they came. It wasn't easy, but she realized that the more she fought her emotions, the more out of control she felt.

"Grief is much like an ocean wave," she said. "If you allow the wave to take you, it's less draining than fighting against the force of the waters crashing over you.

"Praying to God for my emotional awareness helped lighten the path of grief for me. Whenever I felt emotionally overwhelmed or a bit crazy, I prayed for God to reveal to me what it was that I was feeling and to please grant me the strength to deal with what he revealed. Each time, calmness slowly came over me. That was my daily reminder that I wasn't alone in my pain. God was always with me." Liz figured it out that her emotions were absolutely unstable. She didn't push herself to be rational or try to tell herself that it was stupid to feel this way.

Accept your feelings, no matter how strange or bizarre they are. This is who you are right now. It's all right to be you, and it's all right to feel exactly the way you do.

God, I feel strange and sometimes wonder if I am going crazy. I want to accept these feelings as they come. And I want them to lead me to you so I might fully receive your comfort. Amen.

11

Material Possessions

$\mathcal{W}$hile Cec was a pastor, he received a phone call from a woman whose husband had died four months earlier. She asked Cec to come to her home. When he arrived, it was obvious that she had been crying.

Pointing to three large boxes, two suitcases, and a briefcase, she said, "Take them out of here, please." Her tears spilled over again.

After she calmed down, she said she had gathered all his personal effects. She knew she had to get rid of them, but she couldn't take them outside the house. "I got them to the front door, but I couldn't go beyond that door," she said. "So I called you because I thought you'd understand."

Cec understood. As he reached for the suitcases, he asked, "What do you want me to do with them?"

"Give them away. Sell them. Do whatever you want with them, but just take them."

He put them into his car and drove to the Goodwill store.

One of the things you need to face in the loss of your loved one is what to do with his or her personal possessions.

Liz understood that widow's experience. For more than a year, she kept the paper bag with Davey's fuel-soaked clothes. Many nights, while the children slept, she lay in bed and hugged that paper bag. Although she knew that nothing would bring Davey back, she wasn't ready to part with his possessions.

Early one morning she was finally ready to take the brave step and let go of the paper bag and its contents, but she didn't know what to do with them. Placing the torn clothes in a trash bag, she decided to set them out for the trash collectors. For hours she paced the room as she waited for the weekly trash run. When the garbage truck finally arrived, she stood at the window and cried until, in exhaustion, she fell to the floor. *Have I done the right thing? Is it okay to let go of his clothes?* Deep within her heart, Liz knew the answer, but that hadn't made it any easier to get rid of the clothes.

During the following days, Liz experienced an emotional release

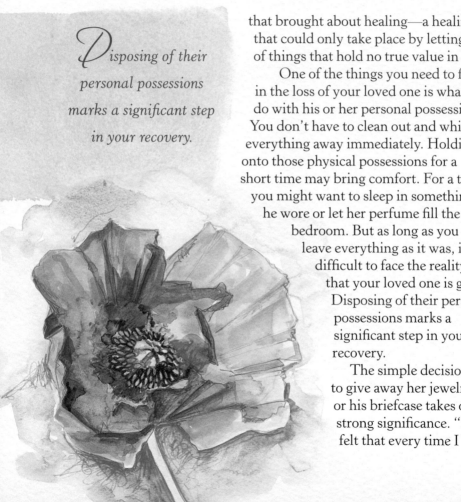

Disposing of their personal possessions marks a significant step in your recovery.

that brought about healing—a healing that could only take place by letting go of things that hold no true value in life.

One of the things you need to face in the loss of your loved one is what to do with his or her personal possessions. You don't have to clean out and whisk everything away immediately. Holding onto those physical possessions for a short time may bring comfort. For a time you might want to sleep in something he wore or let her perfume fill the bedroom. But as long as you leave everything as it was, it is difficult to face the reality that your loved one is gone. Disposing of their personal possessions marks a significant step in your recovery.

The simple decision to give away her jewelry or his briefcase takes on strong significance. "I felt that every time I gave away something of my husband's, I was giving away a part of him," a young widow said. "But one day I realized that was exactly the way I had to do it—I had to give away small parts of him. Each time I got rid of something special—something that belonged just to him—I was getting stronger.

"The decision to give his razor and clothes to a homeless shelter was excruciatingly painful," she said, "but after I came home, I relaxed. It was one small step in my healing path."

The person you loved is no longer here. To clear out that person's belongings is a subtle signal to your heart. That acts says, "I've decided to let you go. I am not going to forget you or ever stop loving you, but I have to do this for me."

God of love, this is a big step, but it's one I need to take. Prepare my heart and make me emotionally ready for that step. Remind me that I'm not betraying my loved one's memory—I'm simply admitting that it's time for me to move on. Amen.

12

Facing Those Special Days

"*I* got past his birthday with little difficulty. I cried quite a bit on the first anniversary of his death," one widow said, "but the absolute worst day was Christmas. For twenty years, he had bought and decorated our tree. Two Christmas seasons passed before I could put up a tree in our house."

When dealing with loss, holidays, birthdays, anniversaries, and special occasions are some of the roughest days to get through. Isn't it odd that one day—one specific day—can send your emotions into a tailspin? Perhaps it's because those around you put so much emphasis on that day. Or maybe it's because you have so many memories tied up with that special day of the year.

Christmastime can be one of the bluest times of the year for those who grieve. For weeks leading up to the first Christmas after her

Things are different, but different doesn't have to mean that they are negative.

husband's death, Liz realized that she was dreading the upcoming holiday. She put off doing everything until the last minute. Anticipating the worst possible response made the situation worse. She envisioned herself in tears and feared she'd spoil the season for her two young children. After going through one heart-wrenching Christmas, Liz said, "I had to find a way to survive the holidays without coming apart."

She prayed for help and asked her friends to pray with her. She tried to think positively. At one point Liz said aloud, "A date is just a number on a calendar." Immediately she answered herself, "If only it were that simple." But she has discovered ways to make those calendar dates good times instead of dungeons of despair.

For example, Liz reminds herself that a special day or a specific date doesn't take away the memories she has of her lost husband. She knows that nothing can bring him back and that it isn't wrong to remember him. She now gives God thanks for the years they've shared. Liz takes the memories and turns them into something special she and her children can remember him by—beyond the date on the calendar.

Letting go of the old way of doing things and starting something totally new can be difficult. The realization that things are different may be painful for you to accept. Things *are* different, but different doesn't have to mean that they are negative. Be creative. Find a new way to celebrate the holidays or begin a new family tradition that works for you. Try some of these ideas:

- Volunteer at a soup kitchen for the homeless on your loved one's birthday.
- Go on that trip you've always wanted to take.
- Take a nature walk and "waste" several hours.
- Call an old friend and go to lunch together.
- Find a nearby chapel or church where you can sit in silence for a time of reflection.
- Get a manicure or do something to pamper yourself.

For example, two years after Davey's death, Liz started a new tradition that has become more meaningful with each passing year.

"Every Christmas I give to charities in the names of my children and in the memory of loved ones we've lost though the years, such as my husband, my grandmother, and close friends.

Find a new way to celebrate the holidays or begin a new family tradition.

"After everyone goes to sleep on Christmas Eve, I place paper angels on the tree. I write the names of each person in the family and the charities to which I gave gifts in their names. On the other paper angels, I write the names of those we've lost and the organizations to which I donated money in their memories. I pick a charity that best suits each particular person. For example, my mom is diabetic so her angel donation is to the Juvenile Diabetes Fund. Davey died of head injuries, so his donation is to the Brain Injury Foundation.

"It's such a beautiful sight on Christmas morning to see the little paper angels with the names of those we love and those we have lost hanging all over our family tree. We pull every angel off the tree limbs and read the names each angel bears and the donation made in their honor or memory.

"The paper angels have become an emotional part of our family Christmas and a meaningful tradition. It started with heartaches—now it brings much joy."

There is no sure way to get through those special occasions, but the best advice Liz can give is this. "Make it your own special time. Figure out how you can pay tribute to the loved one you have lost. Whether it is feeding the homeless or going for a private walk in the woods, your personal way of acknowledging the day is what can make it special."

As you face those special occasions, here's a word of encouragement. "Give all your worries and cares to God, for he cares about you" (1 Peter 5:7).

God of all time and eternity, help me during those special days each year to rise above my grief. Remind me that it's all right to remember those I've loved and lost. Help me make those times special. Amen.

*N*ow may our Lord Jesus Christ himself and God our
Father, who loved us and by his grace gave us eternal
comfort and a wonderful hope, comfort you and strengthen
you in every good thing you do and say.

2 THESSALONIANS 2:16-17